The Call Revolution.

A Radical Invitation to Turn
the Heart of a Nation Back to God

by Ché Ahn and Lou Engle

The Call Revolution.

A Radical Invitation to Turn the Heart of a Nation Back to God

by Ché Ahn and Lou Engle

WAGNER
PUBLICATIONS

The Call Revolution
Copyright © 2001
by Ché Ahn and Lou Engle
ISBN 1-58502-022-2

Published by
Wagner Publications
11005 N. Highway 83
Colorado Springs, CO 80921
www.wagnerpublications.org

Edited by
Karen Kaufman

Interior design by
Rebecca Sytsema

Rights for publishing this book in other languages are contracted by Gospel Literature International (GLINT). GLINT also provides technical help for the adaptation, translation, and publishing of Bible study resources and books in scores of languages worldwide. For further information, contact GLINT, P.O. Box 4060, Ontario, CA 91761-1003, USA. You may also send e-mail to glintint@aol.com, or visit their web site at www.glint.org.

1 2 3 4 5 6 7 8 9   07 06 05 04 03 02 01

Dedication.

This book is dedicated to our children,
holy revolutionaries of the next generation:

Gabriel Ahn
Grace Ahn
Joy Ahn
Mary Ahn
Christy Joy Engle
Jesse Engle
Josiah Engle
Jonathan Engle
Gloria Engle
Jacob Engle

Contents.

Acknowledgments.

Every book requires the culminating efforts of many people, and this one is no exception. We wish to thank…

- Karen Kaufman, our editor, for her expertise and partnership in this work

- Dava Santos and Theresa Noble, our executive assistants, for tirelessly working to keep us organized and on track

- Helena Hwang, Director of The Call, for being a true servant of the next generation

- C. Peter Wagner and his daughter, Rebecca Sytsema, for being willing to rush this book through the publication process

- And, most of all, our loving wives—Therese Engle, the woman Lou calls "Honey," and Sue Ahn, the person I call "My best friend"—for unselfishly laying down their needs to see God's will accomplished for the next generation.

Section I

The Call to Begin.

1. History of The Call.

by Ché Ahn

If you were God and had the power to accomplish anything through anyone willing to yield to you, would you look for someone with self-endowed talents, full of his or her own importance, or would you search for a vessel emptied of self—a pliable person who just wanted to surrender to your purposes and plans? ... I thought so. And that's exactly why God chose Lou Engle!

When I first met Lou back in the early '80s, he was a seminary drop out, mowing lawns for a living. His life, however, was not just about pushing a lawn mower—Lou knew how to push through in prayer. I had never met a person whose life was more reflective of Jesus' example in prayer and fasting than Lou's. So when the Lord called me to plant a church in Los Angeles, California, I quickly recruited Lou and his wife, Therese, to join my wife, Sue, and our children Gabe, Grace, and Joy (Mary would be born in California) as the first members of our church-planting team. That was probably the best ministry decision I ever made.

Lou wasn't gifted as a pastor, evangelist, or administrator, the typical gifts one might look for when building a church-planting team; he didn't even have a marketable skill to rely upon for financial support. But Lou was and is a prophet, and that is why I said, "Lou, I believe that God wants to provide for you to be in full-time ministry in California. Your primary job will be to pray and fast. I'll do the eating—you do the fasting!" Sounds like a perfect plan, doesn't it? I wasn't joking. I loathed fasting back then. As a matter of fact, I still don't like it. But you can't linger in Lou's presence very long without being pollinated with his passion for prayer and fasting.

I have now completed numerous extended periods of fasting, including two 40-days fasts (liquids only)—all because of Lou. Our church has probably fasted more than most, which is not a braggadocios statement. It is instead a testimony to the impact of one man's influence upon a local church—an influence that is now spreading around the world through The Call (a prayer gathering based on Joel 2:15 in the *King James Version*: "Call a solemn assembly").

The Beginning

Lou has always envisioned stadiums filled to capacity with young people gathering for a solemn assembly, specifically praying and fasting for revival. But shortly after the renowned Promise Keepers' *Stand In The Gap* event held in Washington D.C. on October 4, 1997, Lou received a prophetic vision of a youth counterpart gathering at the Washington D.C. mall. Soon he was preaching the vision in youth conferences throughout the nation. In Phoenix, Arizona, the spirit of prayer fell so profoundly upon the young people that they began to cry out for the vision to be fulfilled. Finally, in the spring of 1999, a woman—one who had never heard him preach—asked, "Have you ever considered organizing a massive gathering of youth in Washington D.C. to pray for America?"

Lou chimed enthusiastically, "Lady, I've been preaching that vision all across America."

"Fantastic," she replied, "because I would like to give you $100,000 as seed money to get the vision started." Right there, on that unforgettable spot, the woman scribbled out a check for $50,000. She later mailed him another $50,000.

I'll never forget the look on Lou's face when he came to me as his pastor to tell me the whole story. He held out a check for $50,000 and asked with authentic concern, "What should I do, Ché?"

"Establish an organizational name," I responded. "Then, open a bank account, deposit the money, and find an administrator to organize the gathering in D.C." With loving firmness, I added, "Lou, you know that I will support you in prayer; I'll even ask for an offering at Harvest Rock Church to help fund the project. There is no way, however, that I can be involved—except in an advisory role." Famous last words!

By October's end, Lou still hadn't found an "administrator" and I could see that the burden was taking a toll on him. Not only was he losing sleep, but he was also dropping more weight than he could afford to part with. Within that same time frame, I was asked to minister in San Diego for the weekend. On Friday night, before speaking, I experienced a glorious time in the presence of the Lord during the worship. I wept as I gave God afresh my family, Harvest Rock Church, and Harvest International Ministries (our apostolic network).

I preached and ministered, and it was past midnight before I returned to my hotel room. I was exhausted but comforted in knowing that I could sleep in the following morning. Then, just five hours later, the Lord awoke me with a startling question: "Son, are you willing to drop everything and help your brother, Lou?"

Immediately, I saw flashes of myself traveling for days at a time, away from my family, and raising millions of dollars for a project that I didn't initiate or organize on a national level, something I had no experience in whatsoever. I began to argue, "There is no way that I am going to do this, Lord. You've got the wrong guy."

I heard the gentle whisper of the Lord reminding me, "I thought you consecrated everything to Me last night. Did you mean what you said?"

I knew the Lord had me. Reluctantly, I conceded, "God, I'll do it, but Sue and the family will have to be part of the process. And, Lou and the pastors will have to agree as well."

I flew back to Los Angeles in time to preach for the Sunday morning service at Harvest Rock Church. That afternoon, I broke the news to Sue and our four teens. "What would you guys say if I were to help Lou with the youth gathering in D.C.?" The response was unanimous. Not only did Sue support me, but one by one, our teens also gave their approval: "Of course you should help Uncle Lou."

During that Sunday evening service, I shared with Lou and Therese about what had transpired that weekend. They both started to weep with tears of relief. I often joke that from that point on, I received an impartation from Lou. Now it was I who couldn't sleep and eat under the burden of such a massive project. That is…until the Lord rebuked me in February for being anxious and not moving in faith.

With total support from the pastors, staff, and members at Harvest Rock Church, Lou and I began to mobilize. Our first step was to write a vision statement:

The Call is a solemn assembly bringing together two generations for the purpose of praying and fasting for the revival and transformation of our cities and our nation.

We then formed an impressive Executive Board of leaders that completed the main work behind The Call. Bart Pierce and Jim Cucuzza (senior pastors from Maryland who had organized the Washington For Jesus events) officiated over the logistics with an awesome team of people that included Don Mark, Linda Van Dyke, and Paul Cole. Nancy Duarte oversaw marketing with Cathy Paine, B.J. Anzevino, and Eric Watt, whose team handled the website. Eric also helped me with the media. Rich Manley willingly took responsibility for the follow up, and Tom Smith generously offered his expertise as our attorney. Jim Goll, Cindy Jacobs, and others shouldered the prayer mantle. Bob Gower with Monique Hamada oversaw the incredibly efficient Call staff and its dedicated youth volunteers.

The rest of the Executive Board, which consisted of Bob Weiner, Tom Pelton, Paul Fleischmann, Benny Proffitt, Larry Tomczak, Terry Millender, Guy Carey, Sandy Grady, Kent Henry, Matthew Nocas, Richard Taylor, Patrick Kiteley, Judah Smith, Corinthia Boone, Michael Brown, and Harry Jackson, did a marvelous job of mobilizing the youth, especially on the East Coast. As with any undertaking of great merit, there are always numerous behind-the-scenes workers whose names often go unrecognized to the public but whose efforts have been well documented by the Lord. They share in the inheritance of this unified effort, and words are inadequate to express how thankful we are for each one of them. I am especially grateful to my personal assistant, Dava Santos, and Lou's assistant, Stephanie Telles, for keeping us both on track.

The Day that Changed America:
September 2, 2000,
From Dawn to Dusk

Never have I been more grateful for a fist knocking on my hotel room door than I was on that early September morning. The hotel operator had neglected to record my request for a wake-up call, so had it not been for one of my head ushers, Tom Freers, who came to bless me with a Starbucks coffee at 5 A.M., I might have missed the beginning of a life-changing, history-making day. You've never seen a family move so fast!

When I arrived on stage at 5:30, it was still dark, but it was nonetheless apparent that the D.C. mall was packed with people. Jim Cucuzza approached me with exhilarating news, "Ché, I estimate that there are already 270,000 people here and the report is that the subway is jammed with more people still arriving." A chill shivered up my back.

At 6 A.M. sharp, the gathering opened with my son, Gabe, and John Park leading our youth band in worship. My dad, Rev. Byung Kook Ahn, later prayed in Korean. Both Lou and I had three generations of family members involved that day.

For 12 hours we worshiped, repented, prayed, and were challenged by some of the top speakers in our nation—all came at their own expense. What amazed us most was not so much the program, but the presence of God's glory. Benny Hinn reported that he had never experienced the presence of the Holy Spirit as powerfully as he did that day. Many people claimed that *The Call D.C.* was the most powerful solemn assembly in which they had ever participated.

As awesome as the meeting was on a personal level, we had to remain focused on our primary purpose: to pray and fast for change in America. We had gathered in September rather than a year later (which is what many people advised us to do) because of the upcoming national elections. Our hope was to challenge young people to maintain a 40-day fast with prayer for our nation that would lead up to the elections. Later, when the presidential election made history with its bizarre circumstances and final victory for President Bush, I felt assured that the prayer and fasting of those youth had made a real difference in the electoral outcome.

In the natural, there's no way that we could have mobilized the 350,000-400,000 youth and adults who were estimated to be in attendance that day. The Holy Spirit had performed the mobilization. We could only say, "This is the Lord's doing; it is marvelous in our eyes" (Ps. 118:23, *KJV*).

The Call Continues

The Call D.C. was the greatest ministry challenge that I had ever encountered; it was also my most rewarding ministry experience. When it was over, I was grateful that we had accomplished God's kingdom purposes for our nation. Surely God would say, "Well done, good and faithful servant. Now go ahead and enter into your rest." Sounds good, doesn't it? But I soon found out that what I thought was an ending was just the beginning. Along came Lou with a sheepish-looking grin, "Ché, I believe we're supposed to have other Call events to confront the false ideologies of our society. I feel certain that the next one should be in New England to confront the liberalism in Ivy League universities. I mean, Ché, most of these schools began with a Christian foundation. Let's take back for God what the enemy has stolen. We can do it through fasting and prayer." Why wasn't I surprised to hear that?!

So—as of this writing and with a big "Lord willing"—

we are planning:

• *The Call New England*, September 22, 2001, a solemn assembly to pray and fast for another great awakening while closing the doors on the false ideologies, religious heresies, and intellectual pride that have occupied a portal intended to bring rich blessing to our nation;

• *The Call Hollywood* in 2002, a solemn assembly to pray and fast for the redemption of the entertainment industry;

• *The Call New York* in 2002, a call to repentance for removing prayer from our schools in New York's 1962 landmark case of Engle vs. Vitale;

• *The Call Nashville* in 2002, a gathering to pray for the music industry that is so diabolically impacting our youth; and

• *The Call Dallas*, which is scheduled for 2003 to repent over the Roe vs. Wade decision that occurred in Dallas in 1973.

The Call D.C. has become a catalyst for solemn assemblies in other nations, such as England and the Philippines, as well.

The Lord has promised that "If my people, who are called by my name, will humble themselves and pray and seek my face and turn from their wicked ways, then will I hear from heaven and will forgive their sin and will heal their land" (2 Chron. 7:14). Indeed, our land is in desperate need of healing, and those of us who are called Christians can and should have a part in shaping this nation. But before we can change the land, we must change ourselves. We must answer the call to consecration, spiritual disciplines, and turning from our wicked ways—that is the essence of The Call.

Section II

Core Values.

1. Revolution.

by Lou Engle

"Every man dies, not every man really lives."
—William Wallace, *Braveheart*

"Yes, I believe in God!"—Cassie Bernall's final words before being shot to death at Columbine High School have now become known as the "shot that was heard around the world." In the spirit realm, Columbine is the "Pearl Harbor" of our day to awaken our nation from its spiritual and moral indifference. The martyrdom of Cassie Bernall and others in a once obscure bedroom community called Littleton, Colorado, has set the standard for a revolution—a revolution of righteousness and love launched by Generation X-treme—a generation bearing spiritual weapons of prayer and fasting.

Leading the troops is the world's greatest revolutionary, who never killed anyone. He never threw a rock, burned a flag, or planned a rebellious uprising against authority. He was sentenced to death and went to His execution without struggle or defiance. The power of love, humility, and servanthood ushered in His victory. Jesus, Servant of all, started a revolution that has outlasted empires and civilizations, touched kings, and changed societies. It is *not* a revolution led by violent protestors or angry mobs. No, a thousand times no! It's a revolution spawned out of meekness and purity—out of martyrdom, fasting, and prayer. His revolutionaries are consecrated ones—people separated for a sacred use. In other words, holy men, women, and young people who are willing to lay down their lives for His purposes—those who are willing to confront idols of the heart in order to worship God in purity and wholehearted devotion.

A Pivotal Generation

When the ancient nation of Israel came under God's judgment, a group of consecrated ones called upon Him in the day of trouble. In the Old Testament, those consecrated ones were given a name. They were called Nazirites (or Nazarites).

The Nazirites were a religious order of men and women who arose very early in Israel's history. Scripture indicates that the Nazirite order originated at least as early as the Mosaic Law; it clearly tells us that the Nazirite vow was commonly a temporary endeavor (see Num. 6). God spoke to Moses, saying,

"Speak to the Israelites and say to them: 'If a man or woman wants to make a special vow, a vow of separation to the LORD as a Nazirite...'" (Num. 6:1,2).

God raised up these young men and women to draw attention to the spiritual unholiness of His people and to protest the fact that false gods had captured their hearts. The Nazirites were the Generation X-treme of their day—the Generation Y-zer! They became the role models for their generation.

The period of the judges was a dismal time in Israel's history, so God raised up a new prophetic priesthood that included Nazirites such as Samuel and Samson to help turn the nation around morally and spiritually. Later, John the Baptist, a lifetime Nazirite, would open the door for the ultimate hinge of history, Jesus Christ.

Nazirites! The word *nazir* in Hebrew means consecrated one, separated one, a person of the vow. The Nazirite has a desire, an aching, burning desire to be close to the Lord. Jesus said that of John the Baptist, a Nazirite from birth. In John 5:35 John the Baptist is described as a burning lamp. The true Nazirite is a burning man! The true Nazirite is a burning woman! He or she burns with a passion for God!

The vow of the Nazirite was an extraordinary vow, beyond the normal consecration. It was an extreme response to an extreme burning for God. There's a place in God's heart for extremism. He is moved by extreme acts of devotion. Remember the woman in Mark 14 with the alabaster jar of very expensive perfume, who broke the jar and poured the perfume on Jesus' head? She was extreme in her love for Jesus! She "wasted" a whole year's salary when she poured out that perfume. All the religious people cried, "Why this waste?" And yet, Jesus was so moved by this woman's love that He cried out, "I tell you the truth, wherever the gospel is preached throughout the world, what she has done will also be told, in memory of her" (Mark 14:9).

Extreme love begins with God, while extreme devotion is a response to that love. The Bible tells us that those who have received much forgiveness have much love, and those who have received little forgiveness have little love (see Luke 7:47). God is calling those who have been enslaved by extreme sin,

extreme rejection, and extreme pride to turn their backs on
their former loves and to become extreme for Him.

Many individuals who have been shunned and deemed
as hopeless by the Church will and have become the Nazirites
of our future—consecrated revolutionaries who are called to
lead the war on sin in this nation.

Not Legalism, but Extreme Love

Don't be afraid of being extreme in your love for God. Love
is about sacrifice. It always gets the most expensive thing in
the house and pours it out on Him! O Nazirite generation,
arise! Be extreme in your commitment to separate from the
things that oppose your wholehearted love for God. Do you
love God more than sports? Refuse to watch it for 40 days—
don't even read the sports page, or *Sports Illustrated*
magazine! Do you love God more than entertainment? How
about turning off your TV for 40 days? Say no to video games,
R-rated movies, and Internet pornography. Do you love God
more than sleep? Why not reset your alarm so you can seek
God and pray for an extra hour? Do you love God more than
food? How about drinking juices—except what is from
grapes—for 40 days, expressing your burning desire for Him
through fasting?

"He shall separate himself from wine and *similar* drink;
he shall drink neither vinegar made from wine nor vinegar
made from *similar* drink; neither shall he drink any grape
juice, nor eat fresh grapes or raisins" (Num. 6:3,4, *NKJ*, italics added).

Wine is the symbol of natural joy—grapes, the source of
God-given sweetness and pleasure. For the Hebrew, the en-
joyment of grapes was a legitimate pleasure. The Nazirite,

however, could not, would not, even touch these things. Why? Here's the heart of the Nazirite vow: *These holy lovers of God denied themselves the legitimate pleasure of this life in exchange for the extreme pleasure of knowing God.* We're not talking about abstaining from sin, but good things. You might be thinking all this self-denial sounds like legalism— do not touch, do not eat, do not do! Nazirite friend, this is not legalism—it's extreme love!!!

Choose the Desert of Denial, Not the Decadence of Desserts

Nazirites were to guard their spirits from being drunk with wine. They were to be *possessed* by the Spirit of God. Is God calling you to a special separation for 40 days, or maybe even a lifetime? Do you have a desire to be used by God in an extraordinary way? Begin fasting worldly pleasures and seeking instead the eternal pleasures of God. He will not disappoint you. He rewards those who diligently seek Him (see Heb. 11:6). Set your life course, a course of separation! Then, renew your consecration daily. Others can, but you cannot! You are called to higher purposes—you are a Nazirite!

When God wanted to prepare the way for Jesus, the long-awaited Messiah, He raised up a lifelong Nazirite, John the Baptist. The order of John's life was self-denial: fasting and desert training. Most young Americans, however, are in "dessert training." We've all learned how to feast and play, but the crisis of our times demands that we learn how to fast and pray! John the Baptist's main meal consisted of locusts and wild honey, with fasting in between (see Mark 2:16; 1:6).

It's always the fasting man or woman who changes history: Martin Luther, John Wesley, and Charles Finney. Peter warned, "Abstain from fleshly lusts that wage war against the soul" (1 Pet. 2:11). It's time to humble the stubborn flesh and start doing spiritual weight training so that the spirit can grow.

An Outward Sign
of an Inward Commitment

The hair of the Nazirite was the symbol of his strength: "He must let the hair of his head grow long" (Num. 6:5).

Long hair was a public statement of accountability. It was a public mark of consecration.

People are watching you to see if you live up to your vow. They want to know whether or not your walk matches your talk. The Nazirite walked softly before God and man. Long hair was his *nezer*—crown of dignity! It was God's crown given to him. He dare not cut his hair by defiling himself. God's holy gaze was upon him.

In January 2000, my 13-year-old son Jesse chose to fast on juice smoothies for 40 days, praying for revival and *The Call, D.C.* Toward the end of the fast, he told my wife, Therese, and me, "I don't want to cut my hair until *The Call, D.C.* is over. I am not going to play ball this season. I want to be a Nazirite!" The Bible says there were lifetime Nazirites as well as those who took temporary vows of separation. Jesse wanted to take a temporary vow. For eight months, Jesse traveled with me. Then, there on that massive stage facing a huge gathering of consecrated ones at our nation's capitol, he cried out to God for the Nazirites to arise. The roar of the lion could be heard as the great assembly witnessed the thunderous cry of that young Nazirite's burning heart.

Before that day, however, when my son displayed some bad attitudes, I challenged him, "The hair means nothing if the heart isn't Nazirite through and through." Some of you may grow your hair. That's not what it's about! It's about Nazirites of the heart who love and respect their parents, who bless their enemies, who live their lives counter to a complaining culture. It's about doing the dishes at home with a cheerful attitude. It's about "joyfully" serving your parents. And parents, it's about showing honor to your children. It's about living your vow at home first, then at school or your place of business, and in your community!

Consecration to God brings strength to your soul. When Samson cut his hair, he broke the consecration concentration. Samson literally had his eyes gouged out because he surrendered his heart to his enemy. And yet long before he lost his physical sight, he lost his spiritual vision and wholehearted commitment to God. God is looking for lifelong "longhairs" of the heart. It's time to go public—it's time to live the life of a Nazirite!

Signposts for Life
in the Midst of Death

The Nazirites flourished and multiplied in the days of Israel's spiritual upheaval and moral decay. They stood as resurrection signposts in the midst of the death that surrounded them. They were the countercultural life preservers of the nation. During wicked Queen Jezebel's reign, babies were killed in child sacrifices, the prophets were killed—the culture of death dominated the land. But the Nazirites stood for life. They were not to touch death, or get near it, because of death's connection to sin in the Garden.

"Throughout the period of his separation to the LORD, he must not go near a dead body" (Num. 6:6).

The Nazirites were forbidden to touch anything with death in it, even if their own parents died. Oh, what pressure they must have felt to bury their dead. But no pressure, no influence, no power could induce them to pollute themselves. These were God's pro-lifers!

Are you touching anything that causes you to die spiritually? Are you succumbing to any peer pressure that pulls you toward compromise with dead things? You can't be pro-choice in following God.

The Nazirites were not balanced. The extreme spiritual decline of the times called for an extreme reaction that was marked by holy violence. Every revolution, every revival, reflects the cultural climate of its time. The love and peace of the Jesus Movement mirrored the Hippie Movement of the '60s and '70s. Love and peace, however, do not mark the present generation. No, this generation is infused with a violence that demands a revival of extremism by passionate Nazirites.

A holy war has begun! Nazi or Nazirite? Satan is marching forward with a generation of skinheads, no hairs, willing to lay down their lives for the promotion of death and destruction. But God is summoning a counter youth culture—an extreme generation of longhairs who will sacrifice everything to promote love and life.

Can you hear the rumbles of holy violence? Listen to the words of Matthew: "From the days of John the Baptist until now, the kingdom of heaven has been forcefully advancing, and forceful men lay hold of it" (11:12). What would you be willing to sacrifice for the sake of God's kingdom?

Be assured that your Nazirite extremism will be misunderstood—it will cost you something. Amos 2:11-13 trumpets the message:

"'I also raised up prophets from among your sons and Nazirites from among your young men. Is this not true, people of Israel?' declares the LORD. 'But you made the Nazirites drink wine and commanded the prophets not to prophesy. Now then, I will crush you.'"

Amos warned of a judgment that comes upon a nation when the young Nazirites are forced to drink wine and the prophets are not allowed to prophesy. They say, "You are carrying this too far! Must you fast without food? You have been at prayer meetings every night. Isn't that a little too much?" Parents, allow your passionate sons and daughters to shoot for the stars. Young Nazirite, stay close, however, to the wisdom of those who guard over your soul. Independence and pride will undercut your vow and cause you to become trapped by the vices of the rebellious Nazirite, Samson (see Judges 14-16).

God Only Sends Fire on Sacrifice

After *The Call* event in Washington D.C., my son Jesse came to me burning with passion. "It was worth it, Dad! It was worth it to fast; it was worth it not to play ball." Young man, young woman, do you hear the call of the One longing for the Nazirites? It's worth every subtraction, every sacrifice. God only sends fire on sacrifice!

Have you felt an inward burning for God? That burn is more holy than anything on earth. Treat it as holy—guard that fire. Be willing to sacrifice for it. Ask the Holy Spirit to fan the flames, to set you ablaze with passion, purity, and power! Burn for Him! Join the prayer and fasting revolution! Carry the future of the nation on your knees! You don't have to stand there and watch history go by! You can leap into history this very day and decide to lead the parade with a group of longhaired revolutionaries called Nazirites.

Purpose in your heart that no razor will touch your hair until America is turned back to the living, loving God, no wine will touch your lips until Roe vs. Wade is overturned—until your school is won to Christ, until every public school is able to post the Ten Commandments, until all have been offered the choice to believe that God is the Creator.

When Charles Darwin wrote *The Origins of Species*, he dropped a bomb upon the earth. He declared war on the truth, formulating a picture that all creation evolved from simple matter to complex matter—that humanity was not created in the image of God but that it evolved from a piece of protoplasm, so to speak. The so-called wise of this world believed the lie and foolishly removed God as the Creator from public education. Darwin's theory promotes the belief that: "You're an accident! There's no Creative Designer of your life. You're only the result of natural processes." No Nazirite will tolerate that kind of bogus thinking. Samuel, Samson, and John the Baptist were all conceived in the mind and heart of God long before they were conceived in the wombs of barren women.

Why barren women? Because barrenness shows that God creates something out of nothing. He called the worlds into existence and He called you into being!

It's time for Nazirites to thunder the message in the hallways of every public school, to every kid who wants to commit suicide, "You're not an accident! You're not a piece of protoplasm! God created you. The Designer of the Universe wonderfully and uniquely created you. You've got Designer genes! No matter how good, bad, or ugly the circumstances of your birth, you're here because God wants you here—for such a time as this!"

Loosen Your Locks—Rally the Troops

In 1962, war came to the gates of America and America chose new gods. When our courts outlawed prayer in schools, a vacuum was created and the gods of immorality, Eastern religion, and atheism stampeded our gates. America chose to publicly outlaw the God of our forefathers in public places, replacing Him with the new gods of humanism, the worship of man! Let the Nazirites lead the battle for truth in our nation by setting an example of sacrificial love and prayerfully creating an atmosphere where all will desire a personal, intimate relationship with our loving Creator. Then, the vast army of compromisers will rally and volunteer.

The custom of war in ancient times was that young men would make a vow for victory and begin growing their hair. When the lines were drawn up for battle, these longhairs would let down their locks, revealing their total consecration to death. The loosing of the locks would strike fear in the hearts of their enemies and rally the rest of the troops.

It's time for the Nazirites to loosen their locks for the sake of the gospel, for the sake of America, for the sake of world missions. God is looking for leaders, those who are able to command the timid troops and unite them in massive fasting and prayer for the lost. He wants to see Christian clubs turned from social gatherings to strategic command headquarters and enlistment centers. Nazirites must arise in faith and fasting, in passion and preaching in order to rally the troops and take our campuses for God.

But we must remember that our battle is not against flesh

and blood. We must not motivate people through anger, fear, or hatred of others. We are called to reserve the greatest hate for our own sin. And along with hating our sin comes identificational repentance in which the secret sins of our own hearts are exposed, confessed, and repented for so that we can become the reconcilers of our society. The violence that Nazirites are called to practice is not to be directed toward other "sinners" who are following false gods; it is to be against the pride, envy, greed, lust, sloth, gluttony, anger, and unbelief in our own lives and against the unseen forces of evil through spiritual warfare.

God never handed the earth to the Evil One. The earth is the Lord's. Nazirites are being called to storm and seize the gates of this Philistine culture by heralding a call to extreme love, extreme purity, and extreme prayer and fasting. Who will lead the parade of history on politics, the arts and media, education, science, and music? Will you?

A demonic decree has been unleashed upon your generation! Arise, Nazirites, arise! It's time for a revolution—a revolution of righteousness and love!

2. Repentance.

The Call is a massive solemn assembly of two generations gathered together to represent the Church in prayer and fasting by repenting for the individual and corporate sins of our nation. It is a response to the prophet Joel's resounding summons: "'Even now,' declares the LORD, '*return* to me with all your heart, with fasting and weeping and mourning'" (Joel 2:12, italics added). The Hebrew word for "return" is *shuwb* (pronounced shoob), which means to repent—to turn toward God and away from sin, to change directions completely in areas where our values have been contrary to biblical godliness.

The purpose of The Call is to cause individuals, the Church, and the nation to return to God. It's about refusing to tolerate sin! It's about turning over the tables in places where kids, parents, and governments have allowed the moneychangers to move in and steal our values! It's about reestablishing purity and humility by repenting for our personal sins, the sins of the

Church and the sins of our nation. (The latter is called identificational repentance. See Dan. 9; Neh. 9; Ezra 9.)

The Bible says, "He who covers his sins will not prosper, but whoever *confesses* and *forsakes* them will have mercy" (Prov. 28:13, *NKJ,* italics added). Repenting is more than shedding tears of remorse over wrongful deeds—it is adopting God's heart toward sin, openly confessing sin, identifying with the pain others have experienced because of that sin, and forsaking the sin.

The call to repentance for the injustices and wrongs committed in our nation is not a mandate for the government or our society; it is an appeal to the Church. Judgment begins with the family of God (see 1 Pet. 4:17). So when we, His people, repent for our sins of omission and commission, God responds to our humility by healing the land in which we live. In 2 Chronicles 7:14, the Lord announces:

"If my people, who are called by my name, will humble themselves and pray and seek my face and turn from their wicked ways, then will I hear from heaven and will forgive their sin and will heal their land" (italics added).

God is not saying that a nation or society is exonerated from its sins; He is saying that if His people will repent, then He will send the spirit of revival so that souls might be saved and society might be transformed.

Every gathering of The Call will zero in on a specific hotbed of sin depending on location; however, the following are 20 of the major sins we want to target and repent for at The Call events. Because all sin is serious in God's sight, this list is presented in alphabetical order rather than according to the weightiness of the sin.

Abortion:

The abortion rate in the Church is equivalent to that of secular society. More than 40 million babies have been murdered since the 1973 court decision of Roe vs. Wade to legalize abortion. Scripture unequivocally declares that God takes full responsibility for creating life, no matter what the circumstances of our birth (see Jer. 1:5; Ps. 139:13-16; Gal. 1:15). Therefore, to kill the child in the womb is to sin against God. But the unborn child is not the only victim in an abortion. Millions of youth and adults alike have been physically, emotionally, and spiritually traumatized and exploited by the wreckage that surfaces in the wake of abortion. We must stand against the sin of abortion while bringing freedom and healing to those who are still reeling from its devastating effects. Psalm 106:38 says, "They shed innocent blood, the blood of their sons and daughters...and the land was desecrated by their blood." Only through repentance can we reverse the curse of death that abortion has brought upon this nation.

Abuse:

Emotional, physical, and sexual abuse is a plague in our society. Violent and negligent forms of abuse have enflamed our culture with the venom of rejection, searing people's hearts with an indifference toward life. Husbands and wives have refused to unselfishly provide the time, tenderness, and trust required for cultivating respect in their homes. Likewise, children are resisting the choice to honor their parents. Thus, our schools and playgrounds have become infested with gangs and preteen snipers aimlessly and randomly seeding our land with hatred and violence. As a Church we have been passive and prayerless. We have wounded God's heart by turning a deaf ear and a blind eye to the needs of our nation's victims. It's time to cry out for our heavenly Father's intervention, asking Him to re-parent us as a nation (see Deut. 30;

Matt. 18:6).

Adultery:

Another blight upon the Church paralleling society is adultery. Sadly, reports of infidelity among pastor and parishioner alike are all too frequent. First Corinthians 6:18 states, "Flee from sexual immorality. All other sins a man commits are outside his body, but he who sins sexually sins against his own body." By sinning in this way, every part of a person's life is affected. Not only are body, soul, and spirit poisoned by adultery, but self-worth, personal relationships, and ministry are also minimized. As a spiritual Body, adultery renders us powerless in presenting Christ to a lost and dying world. Adultery has polluted the moral root system in our land, and we are reaping its fruits of unrighteousness. Our nation cannot thrive for long under a canopy of adultery. Revelation 2:22 warns that when a nation yields to adultery, it suffers intensely until repentance occurs.

Bitterness:

Roots of bitterness defile the individual, the Church, and the nation (see Heb. 12:15; Eph. 4:27). Bitterness—which is the spiritual, emotional, and physical toxic root system of unresolved hurts and broken relationships—makes the Church impotent in intercession and prayer (see Ps. 66:18). God is repulsed by our impulse to get even or hold on to unforgiveness. Jesus said that we are to forgive others as He has forgiven us and that we will receive forgiveness in direct proportion to what we have given to others (see Matt. 5:7; 6:9-15; 18:21-35; Mark 11:22-25). Forgiveness is "for" "giving"; it the greatest gift we can give. But we must also "receive" God's forgiveness for our past, present, and future sins. Anything less than complete forgiveness is refusing to believe God, who says that He cleanses us from *all* unrighteousness (see 1 John 1:9). Repenting for the sins of self-hatred and hatred of others is key to revival in this nation.

Division:

God hates division, dissention, and disunity in the Church. Proverbs 6:16,19 states: "There are six things the LORD hates, seven that are detestable to him…a man who stirs up dissension among brothers." D. L. Moody said, "God never visits a divided church." Division through gossip, slander, and church splits is contrary to the heart of Jesus, who prayed that we would be one (see John 17:21). We've been instructed to love our enemies and fight the devil (see Eph. 6:12). Christians need to repent for dividing and tearing down the Church that Christ is building (see 1 Cor. 3:9).

Divorce:

When we say, "I do" with our mouths and "I don't" with our actions, divorce is the result. Nothing has had a more devastating impact on our children than divorce. We have runaway children because we have runaway fathers and mothers who have abdicated their roles in the family. Divorce is the ultimate act of selfishness toward children because it divides the heart of the child. "As the family goes, so goes the nation." War and division within the home has led to riots and gang violence on our streets. By disobeying God's mandate to lay down our lives for our families, we have wreaked havoc upon our land. The magnitude of our selfishness grieves the heart of God. He hates divorce (see Mal. 2:16), but He does not hate divorced people. Let us repent for injuring spouses and children and for the curse that divorce has brought upon our nation (see Mal. 4:6).

Drug Abuse:

Abusing drugs, including alcohol, is not only a sin but also a worldwide leading killer among youth. Alcoholism has become a major contributor to domestic violence in our homes, causing many young people to go astray (see Prov. 20:1). Our nation has opened the door to drug pushers, and drugs have pushed open the door to witchcraft in our nation. The Greek word for "witchcraft" in Scripture is *pharmekia* from which we derive the English word "pharmacy." Drug abuse is an American epidemic. It has caused our nation to become a pharmaceutical laboratory for manufacturing every imaginable kind of demonic activity.

Fornication:

New strains of sexually transmitted diseases among teens are cropping up daily, afflicting our youth with infertility, physical pain, and even death. Sex before marriage is strictly forbidden in the Bible, and yet countless numbers of evangelical teenagers have lost their virginity while professing to know Christ. This frivolous attitude toward what God calls "sacred" is a travesty to Christianity; it defrauds God, self, and others. The Greek word for "fornication" is *porneia* from which we derive the word "porno" or "pornography." It means to pervert God's call to sex. Sex is God's wedding gift to married couples. Opening the gift before its time robs both the Giver and the receiver. God established the boundaries for sex by confining it to marriage. Thus, by exploiting God's gift, moving God's boundaries for sex (see Deut. 27:16) and refusing to take a stand against the advertising and movies used to seduce our nation, we have evoked a curse upon this land.

Greed:

The root of all evil is the love of money (see 1 Tim 6:10). The problem is not having things, but things having us. America was founded upon its trust in God—so much so, that our money is inscribed with the message, "In God We Trust"! But America's trust in God has been replaced with its trust in money, even in the Church. Rather than using money to serve people, people have been used to serve our need for more money (see Matt. 6:24). When performance and products come before people and prayer, the Church becomes an impotent clanging cymbal (see 1 Cor. 13:1). The Church must repent for greed and materialism.

Homosexuality:

Society has so fully embraced homosexuality as a legitimate lifestyle that those who oppose it are labeled "intolerant bigots." Christians believe that homosexuality is not a gender or a race issue but a moral issue (see 1 Cor. 6:9ff). Scripture refers to homosexuality as a shameful lust, an unnatural and indecent act, and a perversion that leads to degrading passions and a depraved mind (see Rom. 1:26-29). As with any other sin, homosexuality can be forgiven and cleansed through repentance and personal renewal. The Church, however, must repent for its indifference to those struggling with homosexuality and for being passive in allowing legislation to pass that promotes and protects what God calls sin.

Idolatry:

Your idol is what you think about most. It's anything you *must* have to be happy. It's what you spend your affection, money, and time on. Anything that comes before Jesus in your life is an idol. Idolatry can encompass everything from reputation and resources to sports and entertainment. Our choices will teach this generation to worship either the living God or the gods of our idolatrous living. Exodus 20:3-5 says, "You shall have no other gods before me. You shall not make for yourself an idol in the form of anything in heaven above or on the earth beneath or in the waters below. You shall not bow down to them or worship them; for I, the LORD your God, am a jealous God, punishing the children for the sin of the fathers to the third and fourth generation of those who hate me." We, the Church, need to repent for hating God by loving our idols.

Injustice:

When you wrong another, you commit an act of injustice. When you are in a position of authority and you misuse authority for personal gain, you are being both corrupt and unjust. When you have the power to do what is right and choose to do nothing, your indifference also becomes an act of injustice (see Matt. 23:23; 25:45). The Church is unjust when it refuses to help the poor and the oppressed of all ethnic backgrounds. The Church has been unjust by remaining silent on behalf of the million plus babies aborted each year. The Church was unjust when it passively allowed prayer to be removed from public schools in 1962. A pastor queried a crowd, "How many of you are angry that prayer was removed from public schools?" Hands shot up in unison. Then he pointedly countered, "How many of you prayed with your family this morning?!" Justice begins in the house of the just, but are we just? "He has showed you, O man, what is good. And what does the LORD require of you? To *act* justly and to love mercy and to walk humbly with your God" (Mic. 6:8, italics added). The Church needs to repent for refusing to act in preserving the rights and freedoms of all who are unable to protect themselves.

Legalism:

This sin is the result of putting law before love. Legalism can refer to anything that exalts the judgments and works of humanity over the complete work done on the cross by Christ (see Jas. 3:13). It ranges from manipulating and controlling others to perpetuating the false doctrine that to be accepted by God and the Church, one must believe in Jesus *and* do something else (e.g., eat certain foods, dress a certain way, pray so many hours a day, etc.). Both the apostle Paul and Martin Luther fought to convince the legalists in the Church that we are justified by faith alone. The Church must repent for the pride associated with legalism, or adding to God's Word (see Prov. 30:6). By making demands on others and excuses for ourselves, we have falsely represented God and caused seekers to reject Him.

Lying:

Lying, cheating, and stealing are detestable to God. In Proverbs 6:16-19 Solomon says, "There are six things the LORD hates, seven that are detestable to him: a lying tongue…a false witness who pours out lies and a man who stirs up dissension among brothers." Lying not only stirs up dissension among brothers on a personal level but it also stirs up dissension among brothers on a judicial level. Lying corrupts trust and divides people. God hates all lying, whether it's coming from Capitol Hill or the privacy of our own homes (see Exod. 20:16; Zech. 8:17). Lying is absolutely contrary to God's nature (see John 14:6; Titus 1:2). It is speaking the devil's language: "When he [the devil] lies, he speaks his native language, for he is a liar and the father of lies" (John 8:44). We must repent for all forms of lying and ask God to restore the spirit of integrity in our nation.

Murder:

The Bible says, "You shall not murder" (Exod. 20:13). God hates "hands that shed innocent blood" (Prov. 6:16ff), because they are hands that have been yielded to Satan. To murder is to take on the very nature of Satan: "He was a murderer from the beginning" (John 8:44). His whole intent upon the earth is to kill, rob, and destroy what God loves—and God loves life. We have become a godless nation; therefore, we have become a nation of murders.

Pornography:

Only a spiritual revolution will reverse the curse of pornography on this nation. It has become a national sin with multi-billion-dollar revenues. Pornographic messages bombard children and adults alike through every avenue of media. Easy access to the Internet has given the devil license to expose elementary-age youth to hard core smut, robbing them of their innocence. Cyber space is now the highway of predators and the byway for new kinds of addictions. Scripture says, "I want you to be wise about what is good, and innocent about what is evil" (Rom. 16:9). We must repent for refusing to protect the innocent from evil.

Pride:

Whatever we derive worth from outside of Christ—wealth, education, talent, beauty, status, etc.—is an issue of pride. Pride is self-reliance, self-protection, and self-exaltation; it is the heart of the independent spirit. It is worship of the unholy trinity: me, myself, and I. God hates pride (see Prov. 8:13) because it separates us from Him. It is the sin that led to the fall of both Satan and humanity; it is also the sin that led to the fall of Sodom (see Ezek. 16:49). Our nation's former bounty is *not* the result of a declaration of independence from our mother country—it is the result of our declared dependence upon Father God: "one nation under God." Many of the curses visited upon our land today are merely the consequences of removing God from our homes, schools, and government. Pride is not the kind of independence our founding fathers had in mind.

Occult:

Sorcery or witchcraft, divination, horoscopes, ESP, fortune telling, Ouija boards, tea leaf reading, hypnotism, mind control, transcendental meditation, yoga, levitation, seances, satanism, and other occult practices were condemned by death in the Old Testament (see Exod. 22:18; Lev. 19:26; Deut. 18:10-14). Our children are besieged with nightly television programs that promote various forms of witchcraft. Similarly, video games have corrupted our youth with satanic imagery and demonic tools of destruction. Because we have bowed to the god of entertainment, the occult has preyed upon our families. It's time to repent and refuse to support evil in our land.

Racism:

In 1962, Martin Luther King said that the most segregated hour is 11 A.M. on Sunday morning. Racism is not only a problem in Bosnia or Rwanda; it is also a core problem in the United States. Billy Graham reportedly cited racism as the major sin in America. The Church needs to repent for *all* forms of racism and anti-Semitism, including its prejudices toward cliques, gangs, and denominations. Our differences should not divide us—they should enlarge us. We are all in this race together; that's why it's called the "human race." Racism is not a skin problem—it's a sin problem, a loathsome offense to God. The sin of racial hatred is a primary root to the violence in our society. What the world needs now is godly acceptance, color-blindness, and unconditional love (see Matt. 22:36-39; Rom. 12:16ff).

Rebellion:
Scripture candidly states that rebellion is like the sin of witchcraft (see 1 Sam. 15:23); it gives Satan a legal right to govern in our affairs. To rebel against parental, pastoral, governmental, and other forms of God-established authority is to rebel against God (see Rom. 13:1,2; Eph. 4:11,12). This is absolutely not to say that we should comply with demands that oppose God's Word (see Acts 5:29). We serve a righteous and just God who holds those in authority responsible for their actions (see Heb. 13:17). But here in America we are a government of the people, by the people, and for the people; therefore, it is our duty to speak up for morality in our land by voting the right people in and the wrong people out. We are to make our voices heard in righteous ways, such as voting and prayer, rather than in rebellious ways, such as criticism and violence. God wants to give us His prophetic perspective rather than our problematic perspective. We repent for all rebellion against authority for our own generation and generations past.

Let's revisit 2 Chronicles 7:14: "If my people, who are called by my name, will humble themselves and pray and seek my face and *turn* from their wicked ways, then will I hear from heaven and will forgive their sin and will heal their land" (italics added).

Notice the word "turn"; it is the same word we looked at previously in Joel 2:12, *shuwb* (pronounced shoob), meaning repent. But turning to God is only a partial definition of this word. It also means to rescue, retrieve, and restore that which was lost. This part of the repenting process is called reconciliation, which is the third core value of The Call.

Let the restoration begin!

3. Reconciliation.

To reconcile is to restore to friendship, to settle or resolve differences, to convert hatred into love, fear into trust. Jesus' primary purpose is to reconcile us to God so that our sin debt will be settled and not be counted against us (see 2 Cor. 5:18-19). Then, because our secret sins have been exposed and openly dealt with, we don't have to pretend anymore. Fear is gone and we can experience His perfect love (see 1 John 4:18). Clean hands and a clean heart make it possible for us to enter into an intimate, trusting relationship with Father God. Hallelujah! But that's only part of the good news. Those of us who have been reconciled to Him now have the privilege of entering into the "ministry of reconciliation" (v. 18). We are to be ministers who help others to resolve their conflicts with God and people.

Second Corinthians 7:10,11 defines the evidence of our repentance and ministry of reconciliation:

"Godly sorrow brings repentance that leads to salvation

and leaves no regret, but worldly sorrow brings death. See what this godly sorrow has produced in you: what earnestness, what eagerness to clear yourselves, what indignation, what alarm, what longing, what concern, what readiness to see justice done."

Reconciliation rests on the heels of action, making restitution for the things we have damaged or stolen. For example, if we have damaged the reputation of a person or a people group, we ought to humble ourselves and make amends in every way possible. Making amends could mean offering a public declaration of truth in order to exonerate the party injured by our gossip or defamation. If we have robbed a person or a people group of dignity, we make restitution by restoring honor. We take responsibility for publicly and privately lifting up those we have put down. If we have stolen property, we make every effort to pay back what we have taken. Scripture says, "Give everyone what you owe him: If you owe taxes, pay taxes; if revenue, then revenue, if respect, then respect; if honor, then honor" (Rom. 13:7).

At The Call events we plan to spotlight the need for reconciliation in five primary classifications of people:

- Genders
- Generations
- Denominations
- Races
- Jews and Gentiles.

Gender Reconciliation

John Dawson said, "The wounds inflicted by men and women on each other constitute the fundamental fault line running beneath all other human conflict."[1]

Since the beginning of time men and women have fought for domination in the battle between the sexes. And though there are casualties on both sides, men have triumphed in the business, political, and even religious arenas. Until most recently, women have only dreamed of rubbing shoulders with those who are fortunate enough to vote and hold positions of leadership in their churches and communities.

Four stouthearted women—Julia Ward Howe, Francis E. Willard, Belva Ann Bennett-Lockwood, and Anna Howard—led a crusade that began in the 1890s and ended in 1920 with the 19th amendment to the Constitution, giving women the right to vote. But the right to vote has not replaced the right to be recognized for the many women who have watched brothers march off to college while they were required to march down the aisle, dashing their dreams and denying their talents. In the '60s many of those same women joined the ranks of the Women's Liberation Movement, burning their bras and abandoning their femininity.

Jeannie was one of those women. She had been molested by an older brother and spent most of her life watching her mother jump, squat, cook, and clean for a chauvinistic father who had little or no respect for women. Jeannie joined a so-called liberated group of discontented women referred to as NOW (National Organization for Women) and began to feed her hatred of men. Eventually she met a guy named Willard with a milquetoast personality and a long fuse for accepting her disrespectful demands. After several years of marriage, Jeannie and Willard gave birth to a multi-gifted little boy named John—and that's when the generational gender pus began to ooze! Jeannie was so determined to protect herself from being hurt by another male that she crushed the spirit of little John and emotionally castrated Willard in front of their son. Willard remained passive but his resentment was none-theless simmering just below the surface. Finally, one day he left without warning, forcing Jeannie to take a long hard look at herself.

Shortly thereafter, Jeannie agreed to attend an Aglow International conference with a friend and accepted Jesus as her Savior. That same day John Dawson, one of the founders of the Reconciliation Movement, pleaded for forgiveness on behalf of the fathers, sons, brothers, uncles, nephews, teachers, employers, pastors, and other men who have acted irresponsibly toward women. His confession was similar to the one in his book *Healing America's Wounds*:

"I may not be the guy that hurt you but I look upon your hurt with shame and embarrassment, nonetheless. Some of you were molested by your fathers, the ultimate parental betrayal. Some of you experienced other forms of incest and you haven't felt whole since. Most of you know what it's like to be the plaything of a teenage boy, emotionally if not physically, and nearly all of you carry some wound of rejection from a broken teen relationship or a troubled marriage.

"You know what it is like to be ogled like a side of beef by someone of greater strength, to be condescended to and joked about in the presence of men. You also know what it is like to be treated tenderly but never taken seriously, your gifts spurned and your advice unheeded.

"Please forgive me, forgive us. You were never meant to experience these things. They represent a gross distortion of the part of the character of God that was to be revealed to you through father, brother, husband, and male friend. These things broke God's heart along with yours.

"You were supposed to be adored by a loving father who praised your accomplishments and cherished the beauty of your uniqueness. You were supposed to feel unconditionally loved and completely safe in the company of male friends and relatives." [2]

Jeannie's life changed that day and so would Willard's. She eventually made contact with her husband and took responsibility for degrading and disrespecting him in front of their son. She also asked Willard to forgive her on behalf of all other women, including his mother, who had tongue lashed him and devalued his feelings.

Gender reconciliation can occur—it should occur—and it will occur when men and women are able to celebrate and honor each other, recognizing that "there is neither...male nor female, for you are all one in Christ Jesus" (Gal. 3:28).

Generational Reconciliation

Malachi 4:5,6 says, "See, I will send you the prophet Elijah before that great and dreadful day of the LORD comes. He will turn the hearts of the fathers to their children, and the hearts of the children to their fathers; or else I will come and strike the land with a curse." Notice the order: As honor flows from the hearts of the fathers (and mothers), it creates a turn in the hearts of the children. Nowhere is the order of honor more aptly demonstrated than in the godhead: Because the heavenly Father honored the Son, Jesus, the Son willingly laid down His life to honor the Father (see Phil. 2:5-11). Generational reconciliation is about unifying two generations through restored honor.

Honor is reestablished when the one who has been hurt feels heard on a heart level with the dual-pronged stethoscope of humility and acceptance. Humility says, "I will stoop as low as I need to in order to get underneath you and lift you up." Acceptance says, "I release all demands on your performance and I embrace all that you are, just as you are for always."

Jesus was so willing to restore the honor of all generations that He took off His heavenly robes and put on the swaddling clothes of a baby born out of wedlock. He allowed Himself to be mocked before the multitudes, rejected before the nations, and stripped of all dignity while hanging naked on an old wooden cross. And He did it all in order to lift up a people who hated Him. His acceptance of society's unacceptable was so complete that prostitutes were transformed into priestly vessels of honor, tax collectors became tithe givers, lepers became landowners, and sinners became saints.

He honored those who would betray Him by washing their feet and promising never to leave them. He did all this to show us the requirements of reconciling love.

As I ponder the words "reconciling love," my soul begins to stir with vivid Technicolor memories of *The Call, D.C.* and the profound impact that day had upon me personally. The dove-gray clouds of morning had lifted like angelic wings to usher in the azure-painted skies that became the backdrop for our day. Then it happened! Because water was in short supply, Coach McCartney asked the parents, youth pastors, and other significant adults to *kiss* the feet of the young people as a symbolic representation of *washing* their feet. Adults and children alike postured themselves in obedience.

With a solemn reverence, my lips became the seal of my love upon the soles of my own children. As I turned to peer back at the sea of young and old bowing and weeping all across that glory-blanketed mall, I caught a glimpse of my 76-year-old, conservative Christian dad, Rev. Byung Kook Ahn. His face shone as he climbed the scant stairs of that unpretentious stage, struggling to steady a large pan that splashed with fresh, tepid water. As he knelt before me, my whole being began to cry out, "No! I don't deserve this." I still remember the feeling of that water pouring over my feet—it felt like liquid love. I simply broke. I could feel the sobs welling up from deep within—waves and waves of emotion bellowed forth.

Until that moment our relationship had been good, but that one soul-shaking act of humility touched me on a level that transformed me. I now realize how humbling it is to be honored and how being honored produces a matchless gratitude in the one who is receiving it. I will never be the same. No one could. That is why God has asked you and me to be footwashing ambassadors upon the earth.

Someone has said that having a child is putting feet on your heart and allowing it the freedom to walk away from you. But when a parent walks away, a part of that child leaves too. Whose feet do you need to wash? Whose feet have trampled your heart? Who has dishonored you so much that you have withheld honor in return? Will you kiss the feet of a generation who have tread upon paths of rejection because of your lack of honor? Whether you are the younger or the older generation, that is what Christ requires of you. Will you do it? If so, you are a minister of reconciliation, and through you, God will bring healing to this land.

Racial Reconciliation

Racism is a worldwide sickness that should never be spoken of glibly. It is *not* a skin problem; it is a sin problem—a ghastly sin problem that is built on fear, which is the character of Satan. Racism stems from being afraid that anyone who is different from me in color, class, or culture might hurt me, diminish me or cause me to lose something I want. As someone recently said, "It's based on "me"-ology, not theology."

The sin of racism is rooted in both inferiority and superiority—flip sides of pride. Out of these pride issues comes a racial pecking order that causes one group of people to kick, claw and kill another in order to elevate their own status and power in society.

Racism is a global problem that knows no national or biological boundaries. Its veins of hatred have bled down through the centuries, causing one generation to become even more steeped in its sin than the last. None of us are born racists; we become racists because of the false beliefs and cultural traditions we have accepted. Racism causes people to separate based on feelings of either inferiority or superiority. Much of what we call "urban renewal" in our nation's depressed cities is nothing more than racial removal. Native Americans, African Americans, Asian Americans, and Latin Americans are some of the most isolated people in our land.

God never asked anyone to separate from others based on race; He only asked His people to remain separated from the idols of others. And He gave that mandate so that He could maintain a spiritual canopy of protection over their lives. Racism is Satan's counterfeit for sanctification. It perpetuates separation from God rather than separation unto God. The word "Pharisee" means separated one, but we are not separated like the Pharisees *because* of our good works (see Prov. 18:1). No! Heaven forbid! We are separated *for* good works. As Christians, we are called to go out into the world, to intermingle, and to draw people to God by our love for all races.

The Call believes that we are to love all the people of the world because God does (see John 3:16). And we love by looking for the best in people (see 1 Cor. 13). Why? Because when we find the best in people, we find God in them.

I once ministered to an embittered young Polynesian

woman who resented her ethnic heritage. Surrounded by Anglo-Saxon neighbors all her life, she felt out of place and different. So I asked her to do a study on the strengths of the Polynesian people and to bring the results of her research to our next meeting. When we met again, her eyes twinkled with a new sense of delight. By accepting her own ethnicity, this young woman was freed to trust God and love others.

God created every people group with a redemptive gift—something to contribute that makes this world a better place in which to live. For example, to mention a few, we see the diligence of God in the Asians, the hospitality of God in the Polynesians, the passion of God in the Italians, the joviality of God in the Latins—every nation reflects a facet of God's beauty and nature. By appreciating the gifts that other races contribute to our world, we also discover our need for each other. And by realizing our interdependence, we tear down the barriers of racism. We were not created to be critics; we were created to be praisers—praisers of God and praisers of each other.

As His ministers of reconciliation, we accept responsibility for our own racial prejudices and the atrocities that have been committed against different races at the hands of our own generation and generations past. It's time to let God break our hearts over the things that have broken His heart—racism, hatred, and pride.

James 5:16 says, "Therefore confess your sins to each other and pray for each other so that you may be healed. The prayer of a righteous man is powerful and effective." Notice the conditions and the promises that this passage offers. We are to confess our sins to each other and pray for each other. *Then*, we—the offender and the offended—will both be healed. *And*, because of our restored righteousness, our prayers will be powerful and effective. That's how we'll win the nations for Christ!

Denominational Reconciliation

I once heard the following precious exchange between a mother and her two children that seems to sum up the matter of denominational differences:

"Mom, are we Catholic?"

"No, son, we're Protestant."

"But, why aren't we Catholic? The other kids in my kindergarten class are Catholic. Is there something wrong with being Catholic?"

Just then, this woman's little second-grader chimed in, "Eric, Catholics just have a different way of showing their appreciation for the Lord than we do!"

It wasn't until 1991 that God personally confronted me with my own lack of appreciation for those who worship Him in ways that are different from my own.

News about the revival in South America had begun to span the continents, and I could hardly wait to drink of its refreshing waters. Then, when my dear friend and mentor, Peter Wagner, informed me about an upcoming conference in Argentina hosted by Ed Silvoso, internationally known speaker and author of *That None Should Perish* (Regal Books), I felt compelled to attend.

Prior to the conference, I had been invited to join some 100 American delegates for an authentic Argentine barbecue hosted by Ed Silvoso. The ranch where we gathered resembled a scene from the Old West television show "Bonanza," and I felt privileged to be there. When dinner concluded, Ed led us in sharing communion and spoke passionately about unity in the Body of Christ. He so clearly conveyed the Lord's viewpoint of denominations, explaining that God sees only one Church. At first, I had at least a pseudo sense that we all saw each other as peers. But I knew the Holy Spirit was rattling my cage to expose the brittleness that had secretly protected my heart. Then Ed led us in a demonstration of oneness that rocked me at the core.

He asked us to huddle together, wrapping our arms about each other to form a human globe. The contrast between the sense of unity I felt at that moment and my inability to see the Church as one simply broke me. I sobbed uncontrollably. God was convicting me of legalism and sectarianism. But that was only the beginning.

Throughout the conference, Ed Silvoso and others continued to speak about unity while I continued to weep. The Holy Spirit was showing me attitudes of competition, jealousy, disunity, and sectarianism. Until that time, I had thought our church was "the cutting edge" of what God was doing because we were "Spirit-filled" and had "the revelation" that He was restoring His Church. I was sure that all other houses of worship in Pasadena where I pastor were missing out on God's best, thinking our "new wineskin" or philosophy of ministry was truly "it"! I repented for pride, arrogance, and comparing our church with others.

At one point during that week, Lou Engle and I took a break from the conference to visit a city named Resistencia that had been tremendously impacted by revival. Church leaders from that city shared how the Lord had prepared them for revival by bringing unity to the pastors. For three years 65 out of the city's 75 pastors met to pray for each others' success and help each other materially wherever needed. I was stunned. Once again I began to repent, realizing how lazy I had been about praying for other pastors in my own city and how selfish I had been in relating to other churches there.

I could hardly wait to get home and make amends for what I had done. From the moment my feet hit the Pasadena pavement, I took off in hot pursuit of bringing unity to the Church at large in my area. I met with every clergy member who opened his doors to me and began looking for citywide events where I could be a vessel of reconciliation.

At one local Concerts of Prayer event founded by David Bryant, I shared a brief testimony of my experience in Argentina and asked the pastors who were present to forgive me for my selfishness and pride. But I also recognized that love is more than words; it's what you do to back up your words. So that Sunday, I asked our congregation to give a second offering that would be distributed to numerous churches in our city. We collected more than eight thousand dollars, which was a large sum for our church at that time. The elders gave me liberty to divide the money into five-hundred and one-thousand-dollar increments for churches representing various denominational and ethnic groups in our community. Some pastors were surprised, others shocked, when I presented the checks. And though we were unable to provide huge sums of money, the difference made by our giving had a *huge* impact on our community.

I have come to realize that just as God has given every race a redemptive gift to validate its significance in the world, so all denominations have an important role in completing God's purposes and plans for His Church. God loves every denomination in His corporate Body and so should we. In the words of a second-grade little girl, "Eric, Catholics [charismatics and Evangelicals] just have a different way of showing their appreciation for the Lord than we do!"

Reconciliation Between Jews and Gentiles

Malachi 4:5,6 is not just about turning the hearts of biological children back to their fathers—it is also about turning the hearts of Christians back to their Jewish roots. The Early Church was not a Gentile church; it was a Jewish church made up of Jewish people. Let us remember that the 12 disciples were Jews; and more importantly, Jesus Christ was born, crucified, and resurrected in a Jewish body. Moreover, He will return to Jerusalem as the Jewish Messiah and "all Israel will be saved" (Rom. 11:26)!

Jesus came to the Jews first and later grafted in the Gentiles. Thus, if it hadn't been for the Jews, we Gentiles wouldn't have a savior! "Salvation is from the Jews" (John 4:22). Think about that. It is impossible to hate your Jewish brothers and sisters and love a Jewish Savior! And yet, that is exactly what many professing Christians have attempted to do.

The early Gentile fathers of the Church subtly and insidiously embraced an anti-Semitic attitude toward the Jews, which still exists in many homes and churches today. We Christians talk about removing the scales from the eyes of the Jews so that they can see Jesus, but let us first ask God to remove the scales from our own eyes so that we can see His love for the Jews.

Countless times I've listened as Jewish adults shared grievous childhood stories of their victimhood—of being slapped, mocked, and pushed around by jaded Christian bullies who labeled them "Christ-killers"! Where do kids learn such absurd nonsense if not from their scaly-eyed Christian mentors? I once told a Jew, "You are one of God's chosen people." He responded, "Chosen for what? Persecution?"

Many Christians minimize the significance of the Holocaust, as if exterminating 6 million men, women, and children was no big deal. And even though there was a physical Holocaust in Nazi Germany during World War II, there is a spiritual Holocaust in the hearts of bigoted Christians in the Church today. It's time to wake up. As you read the following story from *Final Dawn Over Jerusalem*, ask yourself, Who really masterminded the persecution of the Jews?

"If Jesus and his family, all Jews, had lived in Berlin, Germany, in 1940, they would have been prodded into cattle cars at bayonet point and shipped to Auschwitz....

"Jesus Christ, along with Mary, Joseph, James, and John, would have been led into the gas chambers on the pretext that they needed a shower after their long train ride from Berlin to Auschwitz. They would have slowly choked to death on the gas for fifteen long minutes, still standing grotesquely erect because they were packed too tightly to fall. In dying, their bodies would have been covered with sweat and urine. Their legs would have been smeared with feces. This Nazi Final Solution would have been carried out by men whose leaders told them, 'This is the will of God.'

"That night, the skies of Auschwitz would glow red with the ashes of dead Jews, the family of our Lord. Those ashes were often used to make soap or fertilizer for the Third Reich. Think of it! Fertilizing your roses with the ashes of the Virgin Mary, soaping your body with the remains of the apostle John, sleeping on a mattress of human hair provided by the apostle Peter.

"But Hitler and his cronies couldn't see the Jews as the family of Jesus Christ. According to Hitler, Jesus was the first Jew hater."[3]

Jesus a Jew hater? It's mind-boggling to fathom how deceived we can be. Jesus was God, and God loves the Jewish people. He has promised to contend with those who persecute the Jews (see Gen. 12:3). Scripture declares to the whole world, "Israel is my firstborn son" (Exod. 4:22), meaning among other things that the Jews hold a special place of honor in His heart. He also refers to Israel as "the apple of his eye" (Zech. 2:8), meaning that He is extremely protective of that nation. One reason God refers to Israel as the apple of His eye is that everything happening and everything to come in terms of world history can be seen through the prophetic lens of God's firstborn, Israel.

Eventually, the culmination of all prophetic vision will revolve around Jerusalem with the second coming of the Jewish Messiah, Jesus Christ. At that time, the entire world will be sorted into two groups: those who stand with the Jewish Messiah and Israel, and those who don't (see John 5:27-29; Rev. 20:12,15).

God takes our support of Israel very seriously. We are commanded to, "Pray for the peace of Jerusalem: 'May they prosper who love you'" (Ps. 122:6, *NAS*). Notice the promise in this passage. Those who love Israel will prosper. Conversely, those who fight with Israel will be cursed by God: "Whoever curses you [Israel] I will curse; and all peoples on earth will be blessed through you" (Gen. 12:3).

We must love Israel, pray for Israel, protect Israel, and reconcile the world to Israel—because it is in turning the hearts of the children to the Father's heart for Israel that our nation will be blessed!

Notes

1. John Dawson, *Healing America's Wounds* (Ventura, Calif.: Regal Books, 1994), p. 248.
2. Ibid., pp. 246-247.
3. John Hagee, *Final Dawn Over Jerusalem* (Nashville, Tenn.: Thomas Nelson, 1998), pp. 64-65.

4. Revival.

You can't have revival without God's arrival! And I promise you that when God shows up, it will be when you least expect it. Permit me to explain.

It was 1:00 A.M. when my 11-year-old daughter, Joy Ahn, and her friend Christine dashed into our bedroom, shouting, "Take us to Mott! Take us to Mott!" My wife Sue leaped out of bed with a start, instinctively knowing that this was God's invitation. It was the glory of the Lord drawing them to Mott Auditorium, which is the place where our church congregates for services. The girls raced to the phone to ask Lou Engle to meet them there, since I wasn't home. In the meantime, Sue donned her clothes with a flash and quickly drove to the church.

As Joy and Christine stepped over the threshold of the double-doored entrance to that building, their spiritual eyes were opened. The atmosphere was charged with a sense of God's presence while visions of angels burst upon the scene. They both cried aloud with one unified voice, "Mott's too small! Mott's too small! Stadiums will be filled!"

The girls ecstatically described angelic beings, each giving the same descriptions with one unanimous voice. They both saw a ladder stretching from heaven to earth with angels ascending and descending it. Both testified of seeing a man in heaven wearing a football helmet named Vince Lombardi (one of the world's most renowned coaches)! Ironically, neither of the girls knew who he was. Sue and Lou looked at each other with amazement. God was announcing that a Super Bowl is coming to the Church!

We believe this Super Bowl will be a revival that erupts out of The Call and similar kinds of events throughout all nations. We believe that just as youth and adults alike bulge into the overflow of stadiums today to cheer on heroes with nothing more to offer than a game revolving around an inflated pigskin, so the Holy Spirit is headed our way to fan the flames of revival and usher in the presence of the King.

Arrival, Not Just Revival

The Call itself is not the revival; it is merely a catalyst for igniting the purity, passion, praise, and power that will explode when our spiritual eyes are transfixed on the living Lord of love. Real revival is all about awakening to the kiss on our hearts from the Lover of our souls. It is realizing that He is life and all that matters is being with Him. It is loving Him for who He is and not what He can do for us. It is being so enthralled with Him and so aware of His love for us that we are caught up in an attitude of gratitude. We just want to praise Him and in so doing, our voices become the trumpets that usher in His arrival.

But revival is more that just talking about our love; it is

putting hands and feet on it and turning it not only upward but also outward toward the object of the King's love—His Bride. His wife is not a singled-out face, but many faces all wrapped up in one ever-increasing Body, the Church. And the name of His Bride is not one singled-out name; it includes the names of all who are and will become wholly married to Him. Revival is about becoming nameless and faceless in order to celebrate the name and the face of the King. It's about bringing His Kingdom to hollow-hearted people and hopeless situations; it's about getting His will done whether He summons us into a ghetto or a palace. It's about kissing His feet because He has kissed our lives. It's about using our lives to kiss the hurts of others.

Preparing the House for the King's Visit

Revival isn't something we do; it's something God sovereignly does—He shows up! And though we can't force, cajole, or manipulate God into doing anything, we can and should prepare for His arrival. Hebrews 12:14 gives us a key turner for opening the doors to an audience with the King: "Make every effort to live in peace with all men and to be holy; without holiness no one will see the Lord."

Throughout history, the qualities of unity, prayer, and holiness have been the major conditions for revival. D. L. Moody, famed nineteenth-century revivalist, said, "I never yet have known the Spirit of God to work where the Lord's people were divided." Jonathan Edwards said that there won't be revival without extraordinary prayer. And Charles Finney (an American evangelist during the Second Great Awakening, 1702-1895) insisted that revival is nothing more than a new beginning of obedience to God.

Do you want God to show up? Then, clean up your relational messes. Scripture puts it this way in John 4:20,21:

"If anyone says, 'I love God,' yet hates his brother, he is a liar. For anyone who does not love his brother, whom he has seen, cannot love God, whom he has not seen. And he has given us this command: Whoever loves God must also love his brother."

Who is your brother or sister? It might be one of the genders, generations, races, denominations, or Semites we discussed in a previous chapter. But I believe your brother or sister also includes the local Body of believers in every Christ-redeemed church in your city and nation. God is purging the Church of slander, gossip and criticism—and He is so serious about it that He refuses the invitation to visit places where these fiendish attitudes are used as a cruel boot for kicking about His Bride.

Revival will only come with the sword of prayer in the heavens and a towel of outrageous service and love on the earth!

Preparing the Nets

It was during the Jesus Movement that I first heard the message of God's incredible love. I leaped into the net then and never looked back. As a new believer, I thrived in a church that loved me, cared for me, discipled me, and released me into my gifts. But many did not. Numerous young men and women fell away because the churches were simply unprepared to handle the influx.

The Call believes we are about to receive an unparalleled endtimes catch of magnanimous purport. But this won't be a formerly churched group of backsliders or churchyard inquirers—most don't even know the Ten Commandments. This catch will be comprised of an entire generation of fatherless and motherless children who need to be delivered from spirits of suicide, depression, drugs, and violence. They will be the sick and disabled who need a healing touch. They will be the rejected and the dejected who need to know inner healing. They will be the rich and the self-righteous who need to be convinced of their spiritual poverty. They will be the homeless and the directionless who will need to be taught how to assimilate into society.

But how will the Church prepare to handle the harvest? The Church needs to become a hospital for the hurting, a home for families, and a training center for those needing basic life skills. Believers need to be equipped to provide inner healing and deliverance. We need to be a Church that is able to create an atmosphere of nurture and family—an atmosphere of acceptance, forgiveness, and love. We need to create a sense of community in which every man, woman, and child feels as though he or she belongs. We need to make disciples whose lives arc transformed and multiplied through others. We need to raise up a generation who are strong in conviction and powerful in prayer—a generation of holy revolutionaries!

The Bible says that the endtimes Church will be like the Early Church. The "Acts 2" first Church was a temple and a home church, a church made up of small groups, or cells. By incorporating small groups into big churches, every believer had a place to feel celebrated and every celebration became an opportunity to pursue the Lord.

Are you ready for that kind of Church? If so, you're ready for revival—you're ready for a surprise visit from God!

Section III

The Fast.

1. It's Not a Festival; It's a Fast.

In this darkest hour, in which there's no other hope, no other remedy, everything is blight, everything is barren, God says, "Announce a time of fasting; call the people together for a solemn meeting. Bring everyone—the elders, the children, and even the babies. Who knows? Perhaps even yet he will give you a reprieve, sending you a blessing instead of this terrible curse " (Joel 2:15,16 *NLT*).

The extended 40-day fast has far greater power than we have yet realized. If the Christian's fiercest battles are against temptation and the devil, then extended fasting is the atomic weapon in our arsenal!

Great Fasts of the Past

Jesus prepared Himself to overcome Satan by going on a 40-day fast, and many of the Early Church fathers also taught that Christians should follow His example. The men who appeared on the Mount of Transfiguration—Jesus, Moses, and Elijah—had all completed 40-day fasts.

Extended fasting can produce a breakthrough where other methods fail. Elijah's experience with the 40-day fast clearly demonstrates this. In 1 Kings 18, Elijah had just defeated 450 prophets of Baal at Mount Carmel in the presence of King Ahab, and yet he ran like a Nike-clad Olympian when Jezebel threatened to have him killed.

The spirit of Jezebel is always out to kill the call on our lives, but fasting is our protection. Elijah was tracked down by an angel of the Lord and instructed to go on a 40-day fast, which broke Jezebel's intimidation off of his life and prepared him for anointing Elisha—the double-portion son who would carry his mantle into the next generation.

In the informative book *The Prophetic Whisper*, author Richard Gazowsky shares the significance of a 40-day strategy that he received from the Lord:

"'I am going to show you a secret vulnerability in Satan's kingdom. His weakness is in the flies.' Later that day, we went to the Carmel Public Library and looked up the word 'fly'... I discovered that the meaning of Beelzebub, one of the names of Satan, is 'Lord of the flies.' ... Scientists have discovered that flies have a reproductive period that lasts from four hours to over forty days, depending upon the species. When pest controllers go to eradicate flies in a certain area, they spray pesticides every day for a forty-day period. If they destroy the reproductive cycles of presently existing flies, they can kill off a whole generation of future flies. I then saw what God was trying to show me...if a Christian will pray consistently for a forty-day period, he will be able to conquer most satanic strongholds in his life."[1]

Prayer and fasting deals with the demonic powers that seek

to prevail over the earth. If the Church only uses weapons of politics, it cannot gain a spiritual victory. In Daniel 10, we see how an extended fast with prayer removed the demon prince over Persia. Through fasting and prayer, Daniel entered the divine counsel of heaven and learned the secrets of God. Soon King Cyrus was issuing the very decree of freedom that Daniel had prayed in secret!

God is the one who overthrows the edicts of the human race, but He does so in partnership with those who will answer His call to fast and pray. For example, a beautiful young teenager named Esther arose out of obscurity during one of the Jewish nation's greatest crises.

At the urging of the wicked Prime Minister Haman, King Xerxes, ruler of the Persian Empire, gave orders to annihilate all Jews living in the Persian provinces. And with most of the world's Jewish population living under Persian domination, that event would have surpassed the Holocaust of World War II. Clearly, this set up was a satanic attempt to destroy the Messianic line. Nehemiah and Ezra, along with millions of other Jewish people, could have been killed.

Nevertheless, God knew about Haman's evil scheme, and He already had a plan to catapult Esther into a position of influence. Ten years before Haman hatched his diabolic plot, God removed Queen Vashti to make room for Esther. Orphaned at a young age, Esther grew up as her godly older cousin Mordecai's foster child. Then, because of her obedience to Mordecai and humble trust in God, she was entrusted with a position of authority that would save the entire Jewish remnant in Persia. Esther's name means "star" and God caused her to shine in the darkness.

Recognizing that he could not change the decrees of darkness alone, Mordecai (the older generation) turned to Esther (the younger generation) and fasted on her behalf. Armed with the knowledge of the king's decree and a confidence that the King of kings had raised her up for "such a time as this" (Esther 4:4), she was ushered into the kingdom, leading a massive gathering in a national fast.

Notice that once again, in a time of crisis, the answer was collective fasting by God's people. They understood that Haman's decree was a spiritual battle and that the battle could only be won through corporate humility expressed through fasting; they appealed to the only One who could possibly help them.

An Esther Generation

Something happened in the heavenlies at Columbine. It was as though the edict of Haman that had been hanging over America for years had suddenly been made public. The results of unrighteous laws, coupled with a lack of regard for God's holy laws, became clear. And here we are again with a nation, an entire generation, hanging in the balance.

Whether we acknowledge it or not, there's an orphaned generation out there. Metaphorically speaking, this generation is living in pagan Persia. But they have already been positioned by God, and they are willing to be discipled—ready to rise with humility and grace at an unspeakably dark time in our nation's history.

Even as Cassie Bernall followed in Esther's footsteps with her courageous stand, an Esther generation has been brought into a position of tremendous influence before God and the governmental leaders of our nation. Like Esther, let the youth prepare themselves through fasting and prayer for an appearance before the King to plead for the lives of their generation. May they appear before the Supreme Court of heaven to see ungodly decrees overruled in the Supreme Courts of earth.

Could the youth of America believe God for a full reversal of the following decrees?

- 1962 Engle vs. Vitale, a decree outlawing prayer in school
- 1973 Roe vs. Wade, a decree of destruction through abortion
- 1980 Stone vs. Graham, a decree outlawing the Ten Commandments in public schools

A teenager's fast changed history in Esther's day, and a teenager's fast can do it again!

Tips for Forkless Faithlifting

With a call to enter into extended fasts, we must prepare ourselves adequately so that the fast can honor God and fulfill its purpose. The following are some practical tips to help you succeed.

1. Purify your heart for worship.

Lust of any kind is perverted worship, but fasting enables us to cleanse the sanctuary of the heart from all other rivals. We don't fast in order to get something from God; we fast in order to align our hearts with the Father's heart. Holy violence will be needed to battle the pleasures that wage war against the soul, but the result will be greater submission to the Holy Spirit (see Matt. 11:12). During a period of fasting, we can more readily say, "I love you, Lord, more than anything in the world. I would rather sit at your table on a fast than have a feast at the world's table."

2. Take time to pray and read the Word.

Don't allow busyness and distractions to keep you from devotions (see John 15:7). Surrender your fork and pick up your Sword (the Bible)! Matthew 4:4 says, "It is written: 'Man does not live on bread alone, but on every word that comes from the mouth of God.'" Use the time normally spent on eating physical food for eating spiritually at the Lord's table. Spiritual fasts are about dining with God; they're not about grabbing a bite of spiritual fast food! Revelation 3:30 says that God wants to "dine" with you and dining takes time.

3. Have a clearly defined prayer focus.

Scripture says, "Where there is no vision (clearly defined, prophetic prayer goal), the people perish" (Prov. 29:18, *KJV*). Other versions of the Bible substitute "lack restraint" for the word "perish." And Habakkuk 2:2 instructs us to, "Record the vision and inscribe it on tablets, that the one who reads it may run" (*NAS*). In other words, by clearing defining and recording our prayer goals, our prayers won't be scattered all over the place. Scattering is a sign of a curse. Specific prayer goals bring specific answers.

4. Do the fast with someone else.

It's much easier to fast with the support of others. "Two are better than one, because they have a good return for their work: If one falls down, his friend can help him up" (Eccles. 4:9,10). Fasting with a friend or relative provides accountability. It also produces a unity that accelerates our prayer power: "Again, I tell you that if two of you on earth agree about anything you ask for, it will be done for you by my Father in heaven" (Matt. 18:19) We encourage parents and youth to consider fasting together.

5. If you fail, don't give in to condemnation.

The dilemma of "to fast or not to fast" can become a major

tool of the enemy. Even if you fail several times, God always extends grace to start again (see Rom. 8:1). In the words of Winston Churchill, "Never, never, never give up!" If you adopt that attitude with fasting, eventually you will succeed.

6. Parents, consider sexual abstinence for the sake of prayer.

"Do not deprive each other except by mutual consent and for a time, so that you may devote yourselves to prayer" (1 Cor. 7:5).

7. Commit to what and how long you will fast.

- A total fast is without water. Don't go beyond three days.

- A water-only fast is very difficult, but very effective. Depending on weight and metabolism, we can live for 40 days on water alone.

- A fruit and/or vegetable juice fast allows you to enter into fasting but still allows energy for functioning. Most people can participate in a 40-day juice fast. Teens should consider adding protein powder to their drinks.

- The popular Daniel Fast, which consists of vegetables and water, is good for those who must maintain a heavy workload (such as moms and students). Athletes can fast "meats and sweets" if they get protein from other food sources.

8. Prepare physically.

Some people, especially youth, have incurred health problems on extended fasts, so be wise. Consult your physician first to make sure you are in good health. If you do plan to engage on an extended fast, ease into it. Two days prior to the fast, limit food intake to fruits and vegetables only. Fruit is a natural cleanser and easy to digest. Stop drinking coffee and other caffeine beverages, and get mentally prepared for dealing with some crankiness and anxiety. Because your body is working to cleanse itself of impurities, you may experience dizziness, headaches, and various body aches and pains. Refuse to allow your body to detour your spiritual success.

9. Prepare for opposition.
Rest assured that on the first day of your fast, someone will bring donuts to the office, or the classroom. Your spouse (or mom) will also probably be inspired to cook your favorite meals during the fast. You may even begin to have visions of fanciful foods manifesting in your head. Remember: Satan tempted Jesus during His fast. Can we expect anything less? When discouragement comes, press into Jesus instead of the refrigerator.

10. Fast in secret.
Don't let your right hand know what your left hand is forsaking! In other words, definitely do not boast about your fast. Only people who absolutely need to know should be told.

11. Break the fast over several days.
Both the juice fast and the water fast will cause your digestive system to shut down; therefore, it can be dangerous to eat too much too soon. Proceed with caution. Break the fast with several days of diluted, non-acidic juice, then regular juice, and finally fruits and vegetables.

12. Make time for rest and exercise.
While you are fasting, you will want to get as much rest as possible. Take naps whenever needed. Exercise will also help

to revitalize your strength and purge the toxins from your body.

13. Don't limit what you can fast.
If you have medical problems that prevent you from fasting food, you might decide to fast television, sports, shopping, or some other activity that consumes a lot of your time. Then, during the hours that you would regularly engage in that activity, you could spend time in the Word and prayer.

14. Expect revelation from God.
Daniel prepared himself to receive revelation through fasting (see Dan. 10:1,2). Matthew 6:18 talks about a fasting reward: "Your Father, who sees what is done in secret, will reward you." Fasting creates an atmosphere that is fertile for hearing God's voice. He may speak through the Word, dreams, visions, and revelations. Don't limit Him.

15. Don't put time constraints on the breakthroughs.
Often the breakthroughs come after the fast, not during it. Don't listen to the lie that nothing is happening. God rewards every fast that is done in faith.

May thousands of young men and women answer the call to fast and thereby cultivate a greater intimacy with Father God. May they be used in the greatest revival our world has ever seen. Let two generations arise and fulfill this divine mandate. We have taught our children how to feast and play—now it's time to teach them how to fast and pray!

Notes
1. Richard Gazowsky, *The Prophetic Whisper* (San Francisco, Calif.: Voice of Pentecost, 1996), pp. 29-30.

The Call Covenant.

Our Gracious Father and God of all, we thank You for bringing us together as united generations to seek Your face and to repent for the sins of our respective generations as well as the sins of our nation through the precious blood of our Lord and Savior Jesus Christ.

We stand today with hearts united in faith, believing that the Holy Spirit will send forth a heaven-birthed repentance that will empower us to keep the covenants we renew in Your presence this day:

WE COVENANT to love You with all of our hearts, souls, minds, and strength, forsaking materialism, sexual immorality, entertainment, religiosity, and all other idols that would detract from an extravagant affection for You. In humility and led by Your Holy Spirit, we will keep communion with You and others in love, worship, prayer, and the Holy Scriptures.

WE COVENANT as fathers and mothers to wage a spiritual war in prayer and fasting against a culture of death and violence in our nation that has decimated the ranks of our children. We turn our hearts to the children in America, seeking to mentor them in a love for God and their God-ordained destinies.

WE COVENANT as a new generation to turn our hearts in love, respect, and submission to our parents, teachers, pastors, national leaders, and all others in positions of God-given authority. We forgive all those who were in such positions of responsibility when the enemy of our souls released a culture of death upon our generation through the ravages of sexual immorality, abortion, drugs, divorce, and rejection. We commit to obey God rather than man, when the laws of man contradict the laws of God.

WE COVENANT to fight for the life of every unborn child.

WE COVENANT to seek unity in the Body of Christ by rejecting pride, insensitivity, and prejudice, and we pledge to sow forgiveness, understanding, and reconciliation.

WE COVENANT to show practical love to the widow, the fatherless, the poor, and the rejected, as we seek deliverance from religious pride and hypocrisy.

WE COVENANT to promote a spiritual revolution in our nation through a radical pursuit of these covenants and the duties of citizenship—not only voting, but also praying for elected officials. We will pray for the peace of Jerusalem and work for a nation that blesses Israel in accordance with the Word of God.

WE PLEDGE to boldly stand and act on the absolute truths revealed in Your Word, but we reject a religious, critical, and judgmental spirit, because Your mercy triumphs over judgment.

WE COVENANT to invade every arena of our culture with Kingdom love and Kingdom authority instead of abdicating our responsibility to it.

WE COVENANT to reclaim the historic call upon America to send its sons and daughters to the people groups of the earth, fulfilling the Great Commission.

WE COVENANT to fast and pray for a great spiritual awakening in America and the other nations of the earth.

Together we pray the prayer removed from our public schools in 1962:
> "Almighty God, we acknowledge our dependence upon You, and we beg Your mercy upon us, our parents, our teachers, and our nation."

Other Values of the Call.

The Call Will Be Nameless and Faceless

God clearly directed The Call board not to advertise the names and faces of those speaking, praying, or leading worship at The Call events. Although national leaders and musicians will be involved, the focus is not on personalities but on Jesus and His purposes.

The Primary Participants Will Be Young People

Although some parents and pastors will be involved, The Call believes that the youth should be responsible for most of the praying, leading of worship, and speaking.

The Musicians Are to Be Worshipers, Not Entertainers

The Call adamantly believes that participating musicians be invited as worshipers, not entertainers. The Call is *not* against Christian entertainment and concerts, but it recognizes that the sole purpose of these events is to be a solemn assembly for worship, prayer, and fasting for revival. Musicians capable of both worship and entertaining have been asked to exclusively lead the people into worship at The Call.

The Board of Directors Will Not Receive Financial Compensation

Although The Call requires a paid staff to handle

the enormous logistics in organizing events, the Board of Directors, or the Executive Working Board, will not receive any compensation. We desire to be totally above reproach in the eyes of society.

Speakers and Leaders Are to Come at Their Own Expense

So many people are involved in The Call events that it would be cost prohibitive to underwrite every person who speaks, prays, or worships there. The Call also believes that we are to "Gather those who made covenant with God by sacrifice" (Ps. 50:5), which includes the speakers and worship bands. We understand the financial hardship this creates for some, but we are asking others to "sponsor" those who cannot afford to participate without the help of the Body of Christ.

People Should Prayerfully Consider Fasting on the Day of The Call Event

Those who fast should do so under the supervision of parents and doctors and by the leading of the Holy Spirit. A person could fast just one meal or drink only juice for the day. Water will be provided by The Call organization; however, food will not be available because this is a solemn assembly to pray and fast for revival.

The Call is a Grassroots Movement

The Call does not oppose godly advertising and marketing (we do have state and city coordinators for national events); however, the primary vehicle for mobilizing people to gather for The Call events is word of mouth.

The Call Is Crosscultural

The Call embraces all denominations, ethnic groups and various expressions of the Body of Christ, whether Pentecostal or evangelical in persuasion.

The Call Has Definitive Values

The Call supports and endorses all Christian Organizations that espouse its values:

- Worship
- Unity
- Prayer
- Fasting
- Follow Up
- Transformation
- Repentance
- Reconciliation
- Impartation
- Equipping
- Revival
- Revolution

Appendix C

How You Can Be Involved.

The Call offers many opportunities for your involvement through the following avenues:

- Prayer
- Volunteering
- Providing Financial Support
- Getting the Word Out
- Becoming a Revolutionary for Jesus

Please check out the web site at:
www.thecallrevolution.com

Appendix D

Financing the Call.

The Call is financed primarily by the donations of people who believe in its vision and purpose. Many of The Call events will be free and will *not* require registration. However, depending on the facility used for the gathering, events such as *The Call Hollywood* will require registration. Each local event of The Call will also sow a tithe of its fund-raising effort into The Call International in order to support the staff and help other nations facilitate The Call events.

If you would like to financially support The Call, please send your donations to:

The Call
1539 E. Howard Street
Pasadena, CA 91104

Subject Index.